The Colour Nature Library

PUPPIES

By
KATHRYN SPINK

Produced by
TED SMART

CRESCENT BOOKS
NEW YORK

INTRODUCTION

Many theories have been, and still are being advanced on the subject of the origins of the dog. Archaeological evidence shows that from the time that man first lived in caves and hunted for his food, the dog has formed an important and no doubt sometimes demanding part of his family life, but beyond this basic fact we are very largely dependent on speculation. Certainly the domestic dog descended from some very early form of wild dog or wolf, but which form and from what prehistoric animal remains unclear. What is clear however, is that the dog was one of the first animals to become fully domesticated and that for many thousands of years, in return for a few relatively small favours, it has given to man the faithful affection, service and devotion that has earned it the title of "man's best friend".

That this friendship is indeed a long-standing and almost universal one is shown by the very earliest cultures. So attached were the ancient Egyptians to their early breeds of domesticated dog, that the death of one of these creatures was lamented with great pomp and ceremony. The body was carefully embalmed, placed in a specially constructed tomb and finally laid to rest in graveyards specifically set aside for the purpose. The Romans too, recognised the value of these devoted companions. Dogs were brought from all over the world to perform a variety of tasks at the time of the Empire; and we have only to look to mythology to witness the deference awarded by the ancient Greeks to the vigilance and dedication of the dog. It is to the giant mastiff, Cerberes, that the onerous and all important task of guarding the gates of Hades is entrusted.

From early myths to the modern era of that intrepid film star 'Lassie', the dog features prominently in many tales of courage and selfless devotion in the service of man, of steadfastness and perseverance, of attentiveness and concern for its master. Dogs have been bred for many special tasks: for hunting, guarding, herding, draughting, guiding…but most popularly for companionship and as a household pet. The tragic lament "The more I see of my fellow men, the more I like my dog" is heard all too frequently today. The dog supplies unquestioning love and devotion where it is much needed. It brings comfort to those who are distressed, companionship to the lonely and reliability in a world of fluctuating fortunes. For these and a multitude of other reasons, in defiance of 'rational' considerations such as those of finance or the responsibility involved, modern man like his predecessors chooses to take into his home, what in practical terms may well amount to another liability, another mouth to feed: a dog or possibly even more frequently, a puppy!

A puppy of almost any imaginable breed is very appealing. The new-born pup, blind, deaf and consequently largely isolated from the external world might be considered generally lacking in charm and even uninteresting. Nevertheless, by the time, after about fourteen days, that the eyes first open, this tiny creature has already assumed the look of plaintive appeal that so many of us find irresistible. When, during the third week its ungainly wriggling and crawling develops into a highly comical, unsteady walk and with its sharpened senses and newly acquired teeth it begins to make identifiable, albeit sometimes painful responses to human approaches, the spell is already cast. So effective is the enchantment that in cuddling a warm bundle of tumbling fur, the fact that a young puppy may require as much care and attention as its human counterpart may be forgotten. It is only when the bright, happy little thing, removed from its brothers and sisters and plunged into a strange, cold world, becomes a miserable, whining animal that yelps continuously through the night, soils the best carpet and gnaws its way systematically through table legs, slippers and the Sunday joint, that the magic wears thin. In the majority of instances however, it never entirely disappears, for these are only temporary set-backs. A puppy, if handled with understanding and in a responsible way, can with relative ease be persuaded that the middle of the night is not the time for choir practice, that it is just as much fun to dig holes in the garden as it is to make unsuccessful attempts at burying things under the carpet, and even, that the well-stripped bone that remains on Monday morning is far more desirable than Sunday's carefully cooked beef.

That there are instances where puppy charm does not prove irresistible is indisputable. The number of puppies, which are purchased on Christmas Eve and extracted with cries of glee from stockings on Christmas morning, only to eventually find themselves celebrating the New Year, hungry, alone and shivering in the frosted streets bears witness to this all too tragic fact. To the person who has not undertaken puppy-ownership too lightly however, the watering, hurt and somehow understanding eyes that greet hysterical outbursts provoked by puddles under the bed or the half-chewed remnants of a favourite pair of gloves, partly compensate for any minor catastrophes.

The ideal time to become the proud owner of a puppy is believed to be when it has acquired the maturity and independence of spirit that comes with being a full eight weeks old. The time to start serious training is often considered to be at about six months when the puppy is sexually mature. To neglect discipline and basic training in the interim period however, is inadvisable, even foolish. The kind of behaviour which may be viewed, if not with approval, at least with indulgence in nine or ten inches of wriggling helplessness is by no means as acceptable in, for example, a fully grown Alsatian. This then, is the point at which to establish kindly but firmly the foundations of the relationship of mutual trust, respect and affection which has linked man and dog for thousands of years. Doubtless this will involve some effort but the justification for this effort needs no explanation. The pictures that follow cannot fail to speak for themselves.

Left: With the appealing eyes and pendulous ears that lend themselves so readily to caricature…a Basset Hound.

The West Highland White Terrier *on these pages* is the only all-white Scottish breed and a native of Argyll, originally intended to work the difficult terrain of the Western Highlands. Today these terriers perform the less arduous role of affectionate family pets: a pup and its mother *below* befriend a young Cocker Spaniel.

Overleaf: Blue Roan Cocker Spaniel pups.

Retrievers in general are characterized by enviably water-resistant coats, a keen sense of smell and 'soft' mouths that do not damage game. The Golden Retriever *on these pages* is particularly noted for its gentleness, intelligence and willingness to work. It is because of qualities such as these that it has been so successfully trained as a guide dog for the blind.

The puppy with the plaintive expression *left*, with its rounded head, floppy ears and silky soft coat, will eventually develop into a dignified, sturdily built Cocker Spaniel.

The two Jack Russell Terrier pups *right* are descendants of a strain built up by Rev. John Russell, intended to run with his hounds, go to ground and bolt a fox from the rocky crannies of Exmoor.

The distinctive features of the Bloodhound *below* are carried with all the dignity that comes with ancient lineage. They descend from a breed introduced into England by William the Conqueror and used successively as a hunting dog for red deer by William Rufus, patrol dog by the medieval curfewmen and later as a tracking dog by the Police.

The origins of the Welsh Corgi *on these pages* are veiled in antiquity, but it appears to be closely related to the cattle-dog mentioned in the old laws of Wales codified in 920. Today Corgis are known throughout the world and, helped no doubt by Royal patronage, have become popular pets.

The Alsatian or German Shepherd Dog only came into existence in its present form in about 1899 when Rittmeister von Stephanitz supervised the inter-breeding of three ancient strains of European shepherd dogs. The result was a combination of beauty and brains which has made it the star of numerous films and an indispensable assistant to police forces and armed services throughout the world.

It is less than a hundred years since the small and shorter-bodied spaniels officially distinguished themselves from the Field and Springer spaniels to become Cockers. With their long lobular ears and constantly wagging tails Cocker Spaniels have since proved to be such charming and endearing companions that few are now trained to the gun.

Left: Shetland Sheepdogs.

Above left: Old English Sheepdogs.

Above: Collie Cross pup.

Right: Apricot Poodle pups.

Below: Miniature Poodle.

Left: Pembroke Corgi pups.

Above: Collie

The Shetland Sheepdog *above right, below* and posing *below right* with a young Pekingese, bears a strong resemblance to a small Collie and moves with a daintiness that has earned it the Zetland dialect name of 'peerie' or fairy dog.

Left: Rough-coated Basset or Griffon ven Deen.

Above: Alsatian pup.

Right: A mongrel which, despite its lack of pedigree, nevertheless has its own distinctive charm.

Below: Smooth-haired Dachshund.

Above and right: Young Boxers.

Above left: Foxhound pups.

Centre left: Beagle pups.

Below left: Jack Russell Terrier pups.

Below: Beagle and Jack Russell Terrier pups.

Dalmatians first came to Britain in the 18th century, when it was intended that they should act as guardians of the Royal Mail coaches. Because of their air of elegant distinction however, they soon became an essential part of the fashionable equipages of high society. The arrival of the internal combustion engine made them redundant in their working role and now these dogs are simply pleasant and sometimes sporting companions.

Overleaf: Irish Setter pups.

Left: Irish Setter pups.

Above, right and below: Sealyham Terrier pups. Of all the breeds to come from Wales the Sealyham is possibly the most popular, despite the fact that it was originally intended to be particularly fierce for badger-baiting.

Below left: Long-haired Dachshund. An ideal little house dog, although inclined to disobedience!

Above left: Golden Retriever.

Above: Collies, the beautiful and intelligent Scottish sheep-herding dogs.

Right: Samoyed pups. Nicknamed 'smiling dogs', these are some of the most attractive members of the Spitz family.

Below: Bulldogs. Although once used for bull baiting these stocky little dogs have been unjustly nicknamed 'sourmugs' for they are good natured creatures that appear to have suffered rather badly at the hands of breeders.

Below left: Salukis or Gazelle dogs are members of the Gazehound family, so called because they see rather than scent their prey.

Centre left: Afghan Hounds. These native hounds of Afghanistan belong to one of the oldest branches of the Greyhound family.

The solemn-faced Saint Bernard probably has its origins in the mastiff-like dogs introduced from Asia to Europe by the Romans. In the late 17th century they were brought to a hospice in the Swiss Alps founded by St Bernard de Menthon and there performed the devoted service as pathfinders and rescuers for which they are renowned. Most famous of these hospice dogs was Barry, who reportedly saved 40 people before his death in the early 1800s.

The first Lhasa Apsos *above and right* to come to Britain were brought from Tibet by returning members of the Younghusband Expedition in 1904. The name 'apso' appropriately derives from the resemblance of the long shaggy hair to that of the native Tibetan goats.

The term 'Mongrel' applied to the bright-eyed cross-breed *left* need not necessarily be a derogatory one. Most pedigree breeds have been crossed at some point in their history and this may well be an instance where breeding is not everything!

Overleaf: Jack Russell Terrier pups.

The blue-eyed bundle of fur *left* is a very young member of the ancient and dignified family of Old English Sheepdogs.

The Pyrenean Mountain dog *above, right and below* is an equally powerful and sagacious dog whose ancestors arrived in Europe with the Aryan migration. Originally guardian to flocks and herds in lonely mountain pastures, today it makes a gentle family dog with a particular love of children.

Left: Welsh Springer Spaniel.

Above: Blue Roan Cocker Spaniel pups.

Right: English Setter pups.

Below: Orange Roan Cocker Spaniel pup.

The name terrier derives from 'terra' meaning earth and these dogs were originally used to hunt badgers and foxes, driving or digging them out of holes in which they had gone to earth. As may be seen here, this work demanded sturdy, courageous dogs, small in size: *left and below,* Wire-haired Fox Terriers, *above,* Border Terrier and *right,* Yorkshire Terrier.

The Shih Tzu *below left,* with its remarkable courage and almost comical arrogance of bearing, comes from Tibet, where puppies of this breed were often presented as tributes to the Emperor of China.

These beautiful setters are descendants of a medieval hunting dog, the setting spaniel, that was trained to find birds and then to set (i.e. crouch down) so that a net could be thrown over the birds and the dog. The English Setter *right* combines irresistible charm with working ability. Its gentle, chestnut coloured Irish cousin *left, above and below* is generally like it in appearance, although slightly different in head formation and temperament.

Poodles are not merely ornamental powder-puff creatures but also highly intelligent dogs. Although relatively new to Britain, they were well known on the continent in the 17th century when they were frequently used as water spaniels...hence the name which derives from the German 'puddeln' to splash in water.

It is not difficult to appreciate why Golden Retriever pups *below* are universally loved and no less appealing are the wistful Yellow Labrador puppies *left and right*. It is generally assumed that the Labrador originated in Newfoundland, where its forebears are said to have been water dogs which swam between boats and the shore carrying whatever was required of them. The original dogs are practically extinct in Newfoundland but the Labrador is a widely spread and widely loved breed.

The King Charles Spaniels *on this page* owe their name to King Charles I who was particularly fond of the breed. Their aristocratic little faces frequently feature in paintings of the monarch.

Something like a Pekingese with short hair on the back and flanks, the Tibetan Spaniel *left* is quaintly attractive. In Tibet it has been highly esteemed for many centuries and was usually bred in the monasteries where it was valued for its contemplative watchfulness.

Above left and below: Welsh Springer Spaniels. Slightly smaller than their English cousins and distinguished by their red and white colouring.

Above: Pomeranian pup. Being a miniature Spitz, the Pomeranian has a close affinity with Arctic breeds such as Samoyed. When first introduced into Britain it did not attract much attention but its popularity grew when Queen Victoria patronised the fancy in 1888.

Right: English Setter.

Left: Old English Sheepdog.

On these pages: Golden Cocker Spaniels.

Overleaf: Yorkshire Terriers. As the name suggests these mischievous but charming terriers have their origins in the West Riding of Yorkshire.

Originally a fighting dog used for hunting wild boar, the Great Dane has been bred over the last three centuries for greater speed and is now lighter in build. Excellent guards and companions, they are also very elegant dogs. The Harlequin Great Dane *below* is easily identified by its black or blue patches on a white background.

A puppy of almost any breed possesses a surfeit of charm and the ability to assume those expressions of plaintive wide-eyed innocence that make the more susceptible members of the human race forgive almost anything.

Above and below: Yellow Labrador pups.

Left and right: Golden Retriever pups.

Overleaf: Pyrenean Mountain Dog pup.

First Published in Great Britain by Colour Library Books Ltd.
Illustrations and text by Colour Library Books Ltd.
Printed and bound in Barcelona, Spain.
Published by Crescent Books, a division of Crown Publishers Inc.
All rights reserved.
Library of Congress Catalogue Card No. 79-50710

Dep.Leg. B-41.841-85